KU-264-776

John Foster and Korky Paul

# Pet Poems

OXFORD
UNIVERSITY PRESS

## Acknowledgements

We are grateful to the authors for permission to include the following poems, all of which are published for the first time in this collection:

**Mandy Coe**: 'Runs-Like-the-Wind', copyright © Mandy Coe 2000;
**Penny Dolan**: 'Two Old Dogs', copyright © Penny Dolan 2000;
**Gina Douthwaite**: 'Why', copyright © Gina Douthwaite 2000;
**John Foster**: 'Never Poke an Alligator', copyright © John Foster 2000;
**Jean Kenward**: 'The Surprise', copyright © Jean Kenward 2000;
**Wendy Larmont**: 'Snapper Trapper', copyright © Wendy Larmont 2000;
**Michaela Morgan**: 'Escapades', copyright © Michaela Morgan 2000;
**Brian Moses**: 'At the Vet's', copyright © Brian Moses 2000;
**Jack Ousbey**: 'My Cyber Pet', and 'Mog', both copyright © Jack Ousbey 2000;
**Sue Palmer**: 'My Vulture', copyright © Sue Palmer 2000;
**Marian Swinger**: 'High Rise Horror', 'The Phantom Pet', 'Peculiar Pets', and 'Auntie Lil's Pet', all copyright © Marian Swinger 2000;
**Tom Wilde**: 'My Menagerie', copyright © Tom Wilde 2000.

We also acknowledge permission to include previously published poems:

**John Coldwell**: 'Beware! Beryl the Budgie', copyright © John Coldwell 1992, first published in *The Slack-Jawed Camel* (Stride, 1992), reprinted by permission of the author;
**Emanuel di Pasquale**: 'My Cat, Robin Hood' from *Cat Poems* by Myra Cohn Livingstone;
**Richard Digance**: 'The Crocodile' from *Animal Alphabet* (Michael Joseph, 1980), copyright © Richard Digance 1980, reprinted by permission of Penguin Books Ltd;
**Michael Dugan**: 'A Useful Pet' from *My Old Dad and Other Funny Things Like Him* (Cheshire Ginn, Melbourne, 1976), reprinted by permission of the author;
**Richard Edwards**: 'Miss Antrobus' from *Teaching the Parrot* (Faber & Faber, 1996), reprinted by permission of the author;
**Max Fatchen**: 'My Dog' from *Fractured Fairytales and Raptured Rhymes* (Omnibus Books), reprinted by permission of John Johnson (Authors' Agent) Limited;
**Martin Honeysett**: 'I Wish I Had a Dolphin' from *Animal Nonsense Rhymes* (Methuen Children's Books, an imprint of Egmont Children's Books Limited, 1984), copyright © Martin Honeysett 1984, reprinted by permission of the publisher;
**Wilbur G. Howcraft**: 'The Personable Porcupine' from *More Stuff and Nonsense* compiled by Michael Dugan (William Collins, Sydney, 1980), reprinted by permission of the author;
**Lyndsay MacRae**: 'Mary, Mary Quite Contrary' from *You Canny Shove Yer Granny Off A Bus!* (Viking, 1995), copyright © Lindsay MacRae 1995, reprinted by permission of Penguin Books Ltd and The Agency (London) Ltd, 24 Pottery Lane, London, W11 4LZ;
**Grace Nichols**: 'What Asana wanted for her birthday' from *Asana and the Animals* (Walker Books, 1997), copyright © Grace Nichols 1997, reprinted by permission of Curtis Brown Ltd, London, on behalf of Grace Nichols;
**Colin West**: 'My Obnoxious Brother Bobby', 'Auntie Agnes's Cat', and 'Our Hippopotamus', copyright © Colin West 1982, from *Not to be Taken Seriously* (Hutchinson, 1982); 'Anteater', copyright © Colin West 1984, from *It's Funny When You Look at It* (Hutchinson, 1984) all reprinted by permission of the author;
**Kit Wright**: 'Heads or Tails?', from *Hot Dog and Other Poems* (Puffin, 1981), reprinted by permission of the author.

Although we have tried to trace and contact copyright holders before publication, in one or two cases this has not been possible. If contacted, we will be pleased to rectify the omission and any errors at the earliest opportunity.

www.korkypaul.com

## For Bianca Moxley K.P.
Endpapers by Zoë Paul, aged 6¼

### OXFORD
UNIVERSITY PRESS

Great Clarendon Street, Oxford OX2 6DP

Oxford University Press is a department of the University of Oxford. It furthers the University's objective of excellence in research, scholarship, and education by publishing worldwide in

Oxford  New York

Athens  Auckland  Bangkok  Bogotá  Buenos Aires  Calcutta Cape Town  Chennai  Dar es Salaam  Delhi  Florence  Hong Kong  Istanbul Karachi  Kuala Lumpur  Madrid  Melbourne  Mexico City  Mumbai Nairobi  Paris  São Paulo  Singapore  Taipei  Tokyo  Toronto  Warsaw and associated companies in Berlin  Ibadan

Oxford is a registered trade mark of Oxford University Press in the UK and in certain other countries

This selection and arrangement copyright © John Foster 2000
Illustrations copyright © Korky Paul 2000

The moral rights of the author and artist have been asserted

First published 2000

All rights reserved. No part of this publication may be reproduced, stored in a retrieval system, or transmitted, in any form or by any means, without the prior permission in writing of Oxford University Press. Within the UK, exceptions are allowed in respect of any fair dealing for the purpose of research or private study, or criticism or review, as permitted under the Copyright, Designs and Patents Act, 1988, or in the case of reprographic reproduction in accordance with the terms of the licences issued by the Copyright Licensing Agency. Enquiries concerning reproduction outside these terms and in other countries should be sent to the Rights Department, Oxford University Press, at the address above.

This book is sold subject to the condition that it shall not, by way of trade or otherwise, be lent, re-sold, hired out or otherwise circulated without the publisher's prior consent in any form of binding or cover other than that in which it is published and without a similar condition including this condition being imposed on the subsequent purchaser.

British Library Cataloguing in Publication Data available

ISBN 0 19 276191 9 (hardback)
ISBN 0 19 276192 7 (paperback)

Typeset by Mike Brain Graphic Design Limited

Printed in Belgium

20079107

MORAY COUNCIL
LIBRARIES &
INFORMATION SERVICES
J821

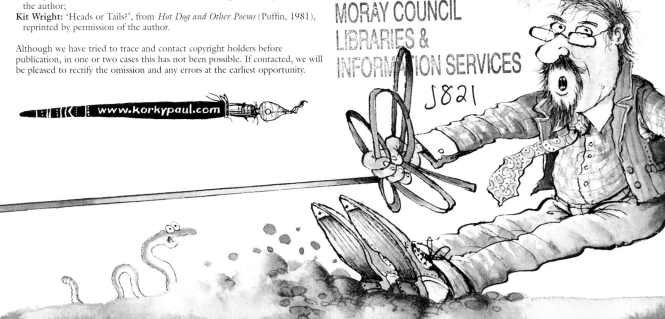

# CONTENTS

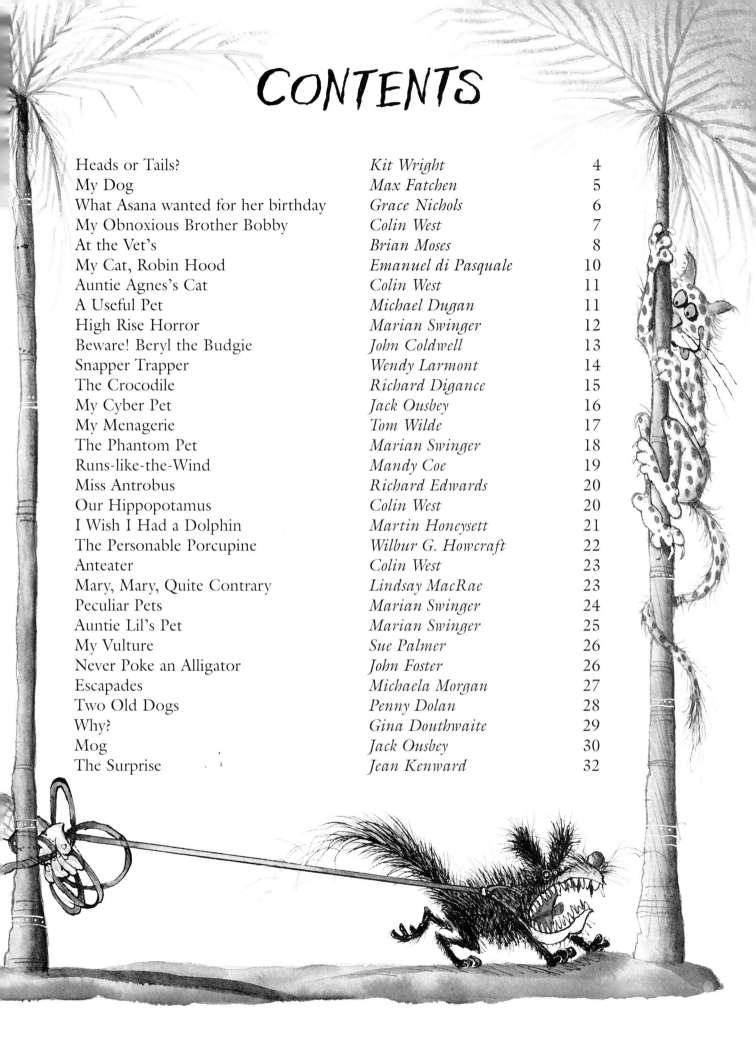

# Heads or Tails?

Dave Dirt's dog is a horrible hound,
   A hideous sight to see.
When Dave first brought it home from the pound,
We couldn't be certain which way round
   The thing was supposed to be!

Somebody said, 'If that's its *head*,
   It's *far* the ugliest dog in town.'
Somebody said, 'The darned thing's *dead*!'
   'Don't be silly, it's *upside-down*!'
'It's *inside-out*!' 'It's a sort of *plant*!'
'It's wearing *clothes*!' 'It's Dave Dirt's *aunt*!'
   'It's a sort of *dressing-gown*!'

 Each expert had his own idea
   Of what it was meant to be
But everybody was far from clear—
   And yet . . . we *did* agree
That Dave Dirt's dog was a horrible hound
   And a hideous sight to see!

 It *loves* Dave Dirt. It follows him round
   Through rain and sun and snow.
When set in motion, it looks far *worse*,
And nobody knows if it's in reverse
   Or the way it's supposed to go!

*Kit Wright*

# My Dog

My dog is such a gentle soul,
Although he's big it's true,
He brings the paper in his mouth,
He brings the postman too.

*Max Fatchen*

5

# What Asana wanted for her birthday

Please don't get me
a hamster or a budgie.
Please don't get me
a goldfish or a canary.

Please get me something
a little scary.
Maybe something
a wee bit hairy.

How about a tarantula?
What's wrong with a spider-pet?
If it gets sick of course
I'll take it to scare—
I mean to see
—the vet.

*Grace Nichols*

6

# My Obnoxious Brother Bobby

My obnoxious brother Bobby
Has a most revolting hobby;
There behind the garden wall is
Where he captures creepy-crawlies.

Grannies, aunts, and baby cousins
Come to our house in their dozens,
But they disappear discreetly
When they see him smiling sweetly.

For they know, as he approaches,
In his pockets are cockroaches,
Spiders, centipedes, and suchlike;
All of which they do not much like.

As they head towards the lobby,
Bidding fond farewells to Bobby,
How they wish he'd change his habits
And keep guinea pigs or rabbits.

But their wishes are quite futile,
For he thinks that bugs are cute. I'll
Finish now, but just remind you:
Bobby could be right behind you!

*Colin West*

# At the Vet's

When we took our dog to the vet's
we sat and waited with all sorts of pets.

There were hamsters with headaches
and fish with the flu,
there were rats and bats
and a lame kangaroo.

There were porcupines
with spines that were bent
and a poodle that must have been
sprinkled with scent.

There were dogs that were feeling
terribly grumpy
and monkeys with mumps looking
awfully lumpy.

8

There were rabbits with rashes
and foxes with fleas,
there were thin mice in need of
a large wedge of cheese.

There were cats complaining
of painful sore throats,
there were gerbils and geese
and two travel sick goats.

There were two chimpanzees
who both had toothache,
and the thought of the vet
made everyone

Shake!

*Brian Moses*

9

# My Cat, Robin Hood

My cat is a tough hood.
He slurps my milk and cereal,
licks my apples and my cookies,
and scratches me
when he's in no mood to play.
He steals my socks
and my baseball cap
and thinks our sofa
is a toy for ripping.

But my cat is also
like a gentle Robin Bird.
He tickles me with his soft tail
and purrs and winks
when I scratch his belly.
He opens the dark
with his bright eyes,
and he sleeps warmly
at my feet on winter nights.

*Emanuel di Pasquale*

# Auntie Agnes's Cat

My Auntie Agnes has a cat.
I do not like to tell her that
Its body seems a little large
(With lots of stripes for camouflage).
Its teeth and claws are also larger
Than they ought to be. A rajah
Gave her the kitten, I recall,
When she was stationed in Bengal.
But that was many years ago,
And kittens are inclined to grow.
So now she has a fearsome cat—
But I don't like to tell her that.

*Colin West*

# A Useful Pet

Leopards, though a type of cat,
rarely make the best of pets,
though if well trained, you may find that
they're useful for collecting debts.

*Michael Dugan*

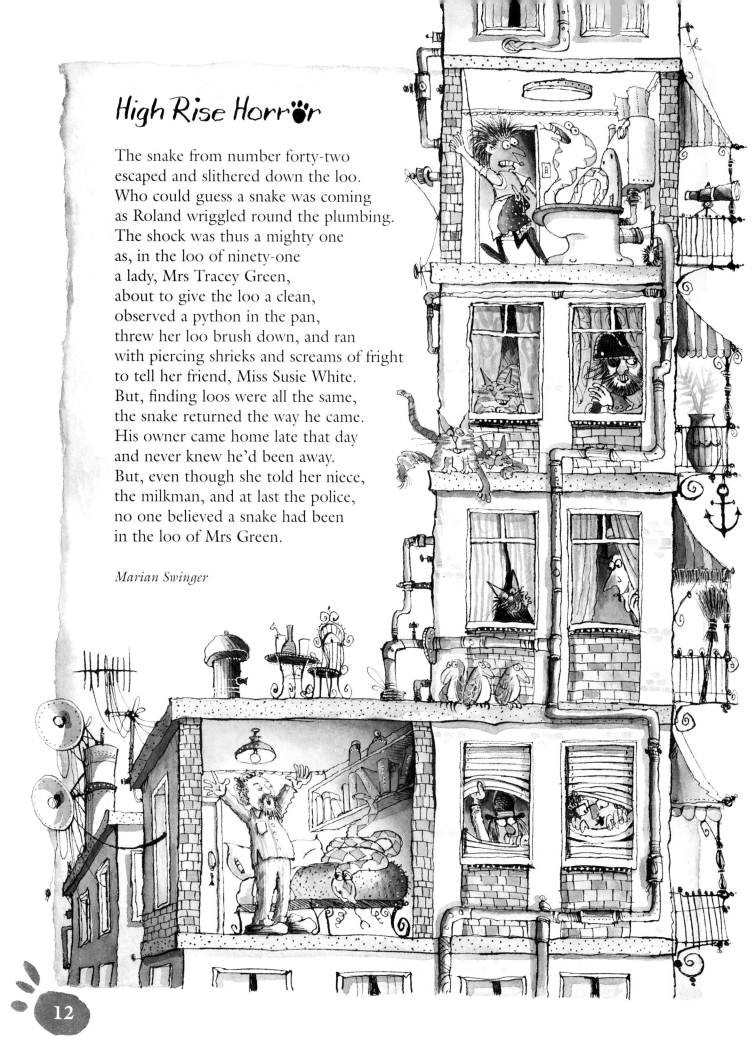

# High Rise Horror

The snake from number forty-two
escaped and slithered down the loo.
Who could guess a snake was coming
as Roland wriggled round the plumbing.
The shock was thus a mighty one
as, in the loo of ninety-one
a lady, Mrs Tracey Green,
about to give the loo a clean,
observed a python in the pan,
threw her loo brush down, and ran
with piercing shrieks and screams of fright
to tell her friend, Miss Susie White.
But, finding loos were all the same,
the snake returned the way he came.
His owner came home late that day
and never knew he'd been away.
But, even though she told her niece,
the milkman, and at last the police,
no one believed a snake had been
in the loo of Mrs Green.

*Marian Swinger*

12

# Beware! Beryl the Budgie

She's a seed eating, bell beating
Ball bashing, mirror smashing
Bully bird. Or haven't you heard of
Beryl the Budgie?

She wears a gold chain and a diamond ring
And carries a pistol, tucked under her wing.
She likes tight jeans and motorbike leathers
Unzipped to the navel to show off her feathers.

If you meet her in the street don't dare to speak
Unless she grants permission with a nod of her beak.
And never suggest that she's broken any laws
Or she'll break your neck with a twist of her claws.

She's done a few jobs, driving getaway cars
She got caught once; did time behind bars
But now she's out and earning a packet
Running a pet shop protection racket.

She's a seed eating, bell beating
Ball bashing, mirror smashing
Bully bird. Or haven't you heard of
Beryl the Budgie?

*John Coldwell*

13

# Snapper Trapper

My brother has an alligator
Hidden in the pond.
He feeds it pies and lumps of steak
Of which it's very fond.

No one knows, apart from me,
He's got it hiding there.
I'm terrified my mum finds out.
She'll go berserk, I swear.

She never let us have a pet.
'We've got no time for that.
You're both at school, I'm working,
So who'd feed a dog or cat?'

But now he's done it, gone too far.
He's pinched it from the zoo.
He made me promise silence
Till he's seen his mission through.

He's got it for one purpose—
If Mum knew she'd have a fit—
To frighten Auntie Doris
When she comes to babysit.

He's planning on such sweet revenge
For those few words we dread:
'Chop, chop now, make it SNAPPY, you two.
Get yourselves to bed!'

*Wendy Larmont*

# The Crocodile

My little pet Crocodile is down in the dumps.
He's had a toothache for most of the week.
He's been brooding about with a sore, swollen snout,
and he's finding it painful to speak.

So I took him down to the dentist last night,
to see if he needed a filling.
The dentist proceeded to climb in his mouth
and in a minute or so he was drilling.

'Ouch,' yelled Crocodile, 'that really hurts,'
as the dentist drilled holes in his jaw.
He was half in his mouth and half hanging out,
so he went through his leg like a saw.

Crocodile told me he couldn't eat men.
I wish he had told me the truth.
The dentist, still drilling in Crocodile's head,
called out that he'd found the bad tooth.

'It's out,' yelled the dentist with his very last words,
'No job is too big for me.'
He then disappeared for the very last time
and the Crocodile finished his tea.

*Richard Digance*

## My Cyber Pet

I bought a little Cyber pet;
I saw it in a sale;
Its case is made of plastic
But it doesn't wag its tail.

There are little coloured buttons
Which make it stop and start;
It's programmed by a micro-chip
But hasn't got a heart.

It buzzes in the daylight;
It buzzes in the dark.
It buzzes when it's hungry
But doesn't growl or bark.

Cyber pets aren't really pets
Just plastic toys that bleep;
If you know a kid who fancies one,
I've got one going cheap.

I'd rather have a puppy
—Though I haven't got one yet—
Yes, I'd rather have a puppy
Than a plastic Cyber pet.

*Jack Ousbey*

# My Menagerie

My favourite pet's my elephant,
though it's ever such a small one.
I've also bought a new giraffe
but it's not a very tall one.

I've got a blue whale, which I keep in the bath,
and a pride of lions who live under the sofa
with a pack of hyenas (which don't really laugh),
and (from the US of A) a short-haired gopher.

There's a herd of buffalo who graze in the garden,
and my grizzly bear's in the shed.
The band of baboons are loose in the kitchen
and a possum's asleep in my bed.

Would you like to see my pets sometime?
They're really quite fantastic.
There's just one problem, I'm afraid—
*they're all made out of plastic.*

*Tom Wilde*

# The Phantom Pet

Our house is haunted. Dad has seen
a see-through gerbil, coloured green.
'It must be George,' our mother cried,
'annoyed about the way he died,
gobbled by that greedy cat,
crunched and swallowed on the mat.'
'Well,' said Dad, 'I'm not surprised.
We'll have to have him exorcised.'
It didn't work. He's with us yet,
a fluorescent phantom pet.
The cat, the cause of all this woe,
has moved next door with Auntie Flo.

*Marian Swinger*

18

# Runs-like-the-Wind

Our rabbit wrote a note to us,
it arrived the other night.
It gave us all . . . a bit of a shock,
we didn't know rabbits could write.

The note was addressed to all of us
but especially to me,
I suppose it *is* my rabbit,
I've had it since I was three.

It's invited us to visit!
*Tomorrow afternoon!*
It said it needs fresh straw and greens,
and '*Could we bring them soon?*'

It says it looks forward to seeing us,
as it doesn't get out very much,
and that we would find it as usual
chewing the wire of its hutch.

We thought the letter ridiculous,
but as if that wasn't enough,
the silly thing signed it *Runs-like-the-Wind*
when we all know its *real* name is Fluff!

*Mandy Coe*

## Miss Antrobus

Why do you love your octopus,
Miss Antrobus, Miss Antrobus?
Why do you love your octopus,
Miss Antrobus, my dear?

I love my octopus because
It hugs me and it wriggles,
I love my octopus because
Its wriggles give me giggles,
I love my octopus because
It juggles jars of pickles,
I love my octopus because
It tickles, oh, it tickles!

*Richard Edwards*

## Our Hippopotamus

We thought a lively pet to keep
Might be a hippopotamus,
Now see him sitting in a heap,
And notice at the bottom—us.

*Colin West*

# I Wish I Had a Dolphin

I wish I had a dolphin,
    It would make a smashing pet,
Maybe I could catch one,
    With my little fishing net.

I'd keep it in the bath at home,
    Though mother's bound to say,
'Get that great thing out at once,
    I've cleaned the bath today.'

I'd take it to the swimming pool
    And ride upon its back.
I'd have to sneak it past the gate
    In a shopping bag or sack.

A dolphin can be very smart,
    So I'd teach it lots of things,
To balance balls upon its head,
    And leap up high through rings.

But I only have a goldfish,
    And he can't leap at all,
He just lies there in his goldfish bowl
    Staring at the wall.

*Martin Honeysett*

21

# The Personable Porcupine

Now a young porcupine
Makes a passable pet,
Though he sneezes and snorts
If his prickles get wet.


So bathe him with caution
And dry him with care,
Shampoo well his whiskers
And massage his hair.


He's tender and loving,
A fair dinkum friend
Whose sweet disposition
I well recommend.


There's no need to sing him
Asleep of a night,
Just tell him a story
And tuck him in tight.


He'll scare away lap-dogs,
Cockroaches and rats,
And frighten the life out
Of unwary cats.


He likes pickled parsnips,
Baked bananas and bread;
But one word of warning—
*Keep him out of your bed!*

*Wilbur G. Howcraft*

# Anteater

Pray, have you met my nice new pet,
An anteater is he.
There's just one hitch—I'm apt to itch
When serving up his tea.

*Colin West*

# Mary, Mary, Quite Contrary

Mary has a little lamb
But she'd rather have a gerbil
She'd dress it up in Barbie's clothes
And paint its toenails purple.

*Lindsay MacRae*

23

# Peculiar Pets

Mother keeps a nightmare
in the stable round the back.
She feeds it all our daydreams
which she gathers in a sack.

Father owns a phoenix
and the local fire brigade
are put on red alert
each time another egg is laid.

My brother has a dragon;
just a small one, pink and white.
It puffs out purple flames
and lights the fire every night.

And me—well, I'm a werewolf
and I've not decided yet
whether I'm their favourite girl,
or just their favourite pet.

*Marian Swinger*

# Auntie Lil's Pet

A pterodactyl came today
and carried Auntie Lil away.
It brought her back this afternoon
which Uncle felt was rather soon.
Looking like a monster bat,
it gobbled up the next door cat.
'Hoy!' the next door neighbour cried.
'Can't you keep your pet inside?'
Aunt's response was automatic.
It lives upstairs now, in the attic.

*Marian Swinger*

# My Vulture

My dad hates my vulture:
He says she's vile and vicious.
But my vulture really likes my dad:
She thinks he is delicious.

*Sue Palmer*

# Never Poke an Alligator

Here lie the remains of Sandra Slater
Who poked her pet—an alligator—
Forgetting that to tease or bait her
Might annoy an alligator.
Alas, the alligator ate her.

*John Foster*

# Escapades

I have no luck with pets.
I had a rabbit . . . but he hopped it.
I had a worm . . . but it turned.
I had a horse but he hoofed it.
And my stick insect . . . wouldn't stick around.

I had a cow . . . but she moo-ved on.
I had a snake but it slipped away.
I had a bat but it flitted.
And my antelope . . . eloped.

I had a greyhound but it did a runner.
Even my bees buzzed off.
My ladylike ladybird flew away home.
And my moose . . . vamoosed.

My fleas fled, my flies flew.
My birds took wing.
My kangaroo took a homeward bound
Even my sloth wouldn't hang around.

So now I've decided. No more pets for me.
Pets are too much bother.
If I want a smelly creature round the house
I'll settle for my baby brother.

*Michaela Morgan*

# Two Old Dogs

Once these two dogs
Tried who could bark the loudest, longest,
Warningly
When people came to call.

Once these two dogs
Saw who could jump the highest, strongest
Stupidly
Up the garden wall.

Once these two dogs
Stole the other's biscuits and bones
Greedily
And munched them in the hall.

Once these two dogs
Chased against each other for a stone
Madly
Or ran away with the ball.

Once these two dogs
Snuck into each other's favourite places
Cunningly
Cushion, chair and all.

Now these two dogs
Snuffle each other's white and whiskery faces
Comfortably;
One beside the other
Grizzled, furry brother,
Half blind, part deaf to almost every call.

*Penny Dolan*

# Why?

Why is his lead hanging on the hook?
His bowl standing on the floor?

His basket is empty.
His blanket is cold.

There's no cheeky bark at the door.

There's no hairy mad-thing to jump on my bed,
to bonk me awake with his nose,
there's no tearing whirlwind to spin on the spot
then run down the stairs with my clothes.

There's no one to share all my secrets,
to listen, while I hold his paw.

His basket is empty.
His blanket is cold.

Why isn't he here any more?

*Gina Douthwaite*

# Mög

Tracy Green says her cat
is the seventh kitten
of the seventh kitten
of a wizard's cat,
and that his full name is
Solomon Sebastian Cat
—and what do we think of that?

Tracy Green says Solomon is a
    deep-thinking, slinking, unwinking,
    cream-lapping, mouse-trapping, cat-napping,
    swift-stalking, slow-walking,
    long-staring, daring, posing, dosing,
    tail-twitching, itching, nit-picking, fur-licking,
    cat-calling, caterwauling,
    autocratic, acrobatic,
    mysterious, imperious
    magical kind of a cat.
And what do we think of that?

We tell her our cat
is the thirty-second kitten
of the nineteenth kitten
of our gran's old stray
and that her full name is
Mog.

We tell her that Mog
can do all the things
Sebastian Solomon can do
—plus one thing he can't do—
she can have kittens of her own
which makes her a
Very Special Cat.
And what does she think of that?

*Jack Ousbey*

31

# The Surprise

'These guinea pigs,' they said,
'don't bite,
they're sisters. They won't
mate, or fight,
but live in friendship
in their hutch,
and not disturb you
overmuch.'

How was it, then,
one morning when
the frost was thick
on stone and stem,
I ran to feed them,
and I found
EIGHT guinea pigs!
They ran around

bright-eyed, smooth coated,
quick and small . . .
Their mum and dad
surveyed them all
with hidden pride
as if to say,
'Who told you
we were sisters,
                 hey?'

*Jean Kenward*